AUSTRALIA

a visual journey across the island continent

ISBN 1-86315-249-0

ISBN 1-86315-253-9

ISBN 1-86315-239-3

ISBN 1-86315-236-9

AUSTRALIA
A visual journey across the island continent

Design Aron Vella / Darren Holt / Rupert Sinniah
Editor Aron Vella / Dan Hormillosa / Rupert Sinniah

Printed by Kyodo Printing, Singapore

Little Hills Press Pty. Ltd.
Sydney, Australia
www.littlehills.com
info@littlehills.com

All rights reserved. No part of this publication may be reproduced, stored in a retrieval system, or transmitted in any form or by any means, electronic, mechanical, photocopying, recording or otherwise, without the prior permission in writing of the publisher.

Little Hills™ and are registered trademarks of Little Hills Press Pty. Ltd.

© 2006 Little Hills Press

Contents

NEW SOUTH WALES 4

WESTERN AUSTRALIA 38

VICTORIA 16

NORTHERN TERRITORY 44

TASMANIA 24

QUEENSLAND 52

SOUTH AUSTRALIA 32

ACT 60

New South Wales

above Countryside near Goulburn in winter

Sydney, the capital city of New South Wales, is the birthplace of the Nation of Australia, and the largest city in the country. The state has breathtaking beaches and coastlines, cityscapes, World Heritage National Parks, snow-covered ski fields, and outback districts.

NEW SOUTH WALES
CITY

Sydney was founded as a penal settlement, but is now a thriving cosmopolitan metropolis. Situated on a harbour that is arguably the most beautiful in the world, the CBD is a bustling area with shopping boutiques, dining and entertainment venues, galleries, museums and historic areas.

Sydney City
below
Sydney has come a long way since the days of Captain Phillip and the First Fleet of 1788. From the Eastern Suburbs, one has a panoramic view of the Central Business District stretching from the Centrepoint Tower, past the Renzo Piano designed Aurora Place to Circular Quay.

City
left
A view of the City over Farm Cove.

Sydney Harbour Bridge
The Bridge is one of Sydney's most famous landmarks. Completed in 1932, the construction of the bridge was an economic feat as well as an engineering triumph. Prior to its completion the only links between the city centre in the south and the residential north were by ferry, or by a 20 kilometre (12.5 miles) road route that involved five bridge crossings.

Sydney Opera House

Commenced in 1957 and completed in 1973, the Opera House is a unique building that has become the symbol of Sydney. It was designed to become part of its environment, and it doesn't take a lot of imagination to see it as something that could sail down the Harbour if it so desired. It has been listed as one of the world's premier attractions.

Taronga Zoo
above

Never before have people been able to experience all the wonders of the world's natural environments so close to the city. The Zoo's new precincts will immerse visitors in a natural and cultural experience.

Cockle Bay, Darling Harbour
top right

Innovative architecture is a feature of the Cockle Bay Wharf development, complemented by the space-age IMAX Theatre at its southern end. During lunchtimes and evenings, people stream from their offices to patronize the many cafes, bars and restaurants found along the trendy strip.

Paddington
right

The streets of this inner city suburb are lined with pretty terrace houses that are decorated with `Paddington Lace', a distinctive wrought-iron trimming. Paddington hosts many antique shops, art galleries, and old-fashioned pubs

City Centre
near right

The city centre, with shops and eateries galore, has skyscrapers for a backdrop. It is a mecca for tourists from all over the world, as well as Sydneysiders out for lunch or in search of a bargain.

Department of Lands Building
far right

The classic edwardian sandstone building of the Department of Lands enhances Bridge Street. The statues of many local explorers grace the facade.

Hyde Park
right page

The Archibald Fountain, with its fanning peacock-pattern spray, captures the attention of people strolling through the north section of Hyde Park. The south section is home to the War Memorial; the western boundary adjoins the commerce and trade district of Market and Elizabeth streets; and the eastern boundary leads to St Mary's Cathedral.

NEW SOUTH WALES
COASTAL

New South Wales is well-known for its beautiful coasts and bays that stretch for 350 kilometres. The beaches boasts of dazzling white sand and surfing waters.

Ulladulla Beach
right

Ulladulla Beach, on the New South Wales south coast, is a tranquil setting most of the year. However, the summer holiday months see thousands of people flock here from the inland and from the north. Australia's coastline is mostly blessed with white, soft, sandy beaches.

Byron Bay Area
above

This north coast area boasts great surfing beaches and a subtropical climate. Byron has been a mecca for a myriad of people, from backpackers and bohemians, to more conservative types.

NEW SOUTH WALES
INLAND

Although the majority of Australia's population is cluttered around the coastline, there are many inland districts that are popular as alternative and more affordable residences. One example is the Blue Mountains area, to the west of Sydney.

Blue Mountains
Katoomba is approximately 110 kilometres from central Sydney, and around 1000 metres (3336 feet) above sea level. It encompasses Echo Point which give views to the mountains and the Three Sisters. Winters here are chilly and summers are mild, while February has the most rainfall.

Echo Point (above)
The lookout at Echo Point offers extensive views of the thickly wooded Blue Mountains, including the famous Three Sisters (above), a popular trio that is important in Aboriginal legends. Throughout the mountains the creeks and fault lines are reflected in the indentations in the vegetation.

Thredbo Creek
The Thredbo River meanders through the heart of beautiful Kosciusko National Park. This area is a playground for skiers during the winter months, and for bushwalkers at other times.

The Blue Mountains
left
In autumn the Blue Mountains are alive with trees of bright reds, oranges and browns. The mountains are dotted with many small towns that have roadside stalls offering fresh fruit and vegetables.

Victoria

above Melboure City Centre

Victoria, the Garden State, is situated in the south-eastern corner of Australia, and well known for its acres of parklands along the Yarra River, its tree-lined boulevards, and extensive gardens. Though Victoria is the second smallest state in the country, it is rich in culture with many festivals. Attractions include wineries, lakes, mountains, landscapes and native wildlife.

VICTORIA
CITY

Melbourne is the capital of Victoria, and is located on the shores of Port Phillip Bay with the Yarra River flowing through the city centre. Stylish and elegant, Melbourne is known as the Fashion Capital of Australia, and is recognized for its interest in the arts, fine food, wine and shopping.

Princes Bridge
below
Trams and cars on one of Melbourne's oldest and grandest bridges, here Swanston Street becomes St Kilda Road. Built around 1886, it replaced an old wooden bridge that had been opened by Lieutenant-Governor La Trobe in 1850.

CBD
below

Melbourne's tallest building and the worlds tallest residential building, the Eureka tower stands at a height of 297m with 92 storeys.

Collins Street
above

A fashion boutique mecca of designer labels and specialty shops. Linked to Bourke and Little Collins Streets, these arcades are solely dedicated to those who seek some serious retail therapy.

Kings Domain, Melbourne
above
South of the Yarra River, many gardens surrounds St Kilda Road and gives a wonderful aspect to this part of the city. The Kings Domain is part of this setting.

VICTORIA COAST

Travelling along the Victorian coastline guarantees stunning ocean views, laid-back coastal towns and villages. The contours of the rocky and jagged south-west coast offer opportunities to soak up the sun and water, fish or whale watch.

The Twelve Apostles
below
The Great Ocean Road travels along the southern coastline and provides spectacular views of rugged rock formations that have been formed by the stormy nature of the Southern Ocean.

Port Phillip Bay
above
Sunset on Port Phillip Bay, viewed from Edithvale south of Mordialloc. The beaches on the eastern shores of the Bay have beautiful white sands, but no surf. This is an idyllic place for a stroll in the evening.

VICTORIA

INLAND

Victoria's inland is natural sheep grazing country, complemented by fruit orchards, vineyards, caves and mountains, heritage buildings, mining towns and abandoned gold mines.

McKenzie Falls
left
McKenzie Falls is the largest and most popular of the many waterfalls in The Grampians.

Bogong High Plains
above

Mt Bogong, Victoria's highest peak, sits at 1986m (6516 feet) above sea level, providing wonderful views of Mt Feathertop and the western peaks.

Mount Arapiles
above

Mount Arapiles rises sharply from the Wimmera plains to form part of the Mount Arapiles-Tooan State Park. The park includes Mitre Rock, the Tooan block and examples of about 14 per cent of the state's flora species.

Country Victoria
above

Victoria is home to large tracts of lush greenery, trickling creeks and majestic mountian views.

Tasmania

above Inland Tasman countryside

Australia's only island state, Tasmania boasts world heritage buildings, relics of its convict past, orchards and vineyards, national parks, rugged mountains, rolling green hills and raging rivers. The extinct Tasmanian Tiger once roamed throughout the state.

TASMANIA
CITY

Hobart is the capital of Tasmania, and the second oldest city of Australia. It lies between the Derwent River Estuary at Stormy Bay and the foot of Mount Wellington. Its architecture is a reflection of its age.

Hobart
below
A view of the city and its environs from Mount Wellington, highlighting the Tasman Bridge and the Derwent River.

Hobart
top

Fishing vessels moor in this area of the port of Hobart as do ocean going vessels. It also is home to many sailing yachts that compete in the Sydney to Hobart race in late December every year. The north side of the dock is lined by National Trust-listed warehouses that are still in use today.

Mersey River, Devonport
above

Thousands of visitors disembark from the *Spirit of Tasmania* at the port of Devonport, which is the fourth largest city in Tasmania. It was originally made up of two towns, Formby and Torquay, however they voted to consolidate in 1893.

TASMANIA

INLAND

Tasmania is known for its tranquil forests and mountain ranges, and old historical towns with beautifully preserved buildings.

Mount Roland
above

Though the mountains in Australia are not high (Australia's highest mountain, Mt Kosciusko, is 2230 metres - 7314 feet), they tend to dominate the landscape.

Mount Field National Park
left

This is a scene of tropical vegetation in an unlikely place. The base of Mount Field National Park is home to Russell Falls and lush vegetation that extends up the valley to the Falls. These are easily accessible by foot, and are close to the entrance to the Park, which is about 80 kilometres (50 miles) from Hobart.

TASMANIA
COAST

The Tasmanian coast is full of many contrasts. In the west, the roaring forties lash an almost inaccessible coastline, creating a forbidding landscape. On the other hand, the east coast boasts tranquil bays, white sandy beaches, accessible offshore islands and wonderful surf throughout the summer.

Freycinet National Park
below
From within Freycinet National Park, this view across Coles Bay looks towards the main part of the island near Swansea on the east coast of Tasmania. Illuminated by midday light, the rich colours of the outcrop reach towards the faint coastline in the distance. Thick, sugar-white clouds fill a slice of Australian sky.

Sandy Bay Marina
above
Yachts remain at anchor in a delightful part of Hobart. In the background is the historical area of Battery Point.

Cradle Mountain
right
Overlooking Lake Dove, Cradle Mountian National Park is some 60km, west of Launceston.

South Australia

above Barossa Valley

South Australia is renowned for its vineyards, and produces seventy per cent of Australian wines, most of which are exported. It comes as no surprise then that it is known as the Wine State. Features of South Australia include the Outback and the sea, and there are many festivals and cultural activities.

SOUTH AUSTRALIA
CITY

Adelaide, the capital of South Australia, is known as the City of Churches. It is a well-planned city with many restored colonial buildings, and many parks and gardens.

Adelaide
The River Torrens flows through the centre of the city, which lies on a narrow coastal plain bounded on the west by the Gulf of St Vincent and on the east by the Mount Lofty Ranges. The Town Hall illuminated at night. (above)

Victoria Square Fountain
left
The fountain is situated in the northern half of Victoria Square between Flinders and Franklin Streets and Wakefield and Grote Streets.
The theme of the fountain is the three rivers from which Adelaide draws its water: the Murray, the Torrens and the Onkaparinga.

SOUTH AUSTRALIA
COAST

The South Australian coast has some areas that offer attractive and enticing beaches; some that are interlaced with mangrove mudflats; and others where the raging ocean waters and rugged rocks discourage visitors.

Great Australian Bight

The Bight is well known as a crucial calving area for the Southern Right Whale, but it also provides a vital habitat for the endangered Australian Sea Lion, as well as other types of sea creatures (eg. great white shark, scores of fish and other whale types).

SOUTH AUSTRALIA
INLAND

The South Australian inland is an ensemble of hills, gorges, valleys, vineyards and mountains.

Homestead
below
The old Post and Telegraph Station at Willunga township.

Clare Valley
above

The Clare Valley is one of the most famous wine producing areas in Australia. First inhabited by settlers from England, Ireland and Poland in the 1800's, a rich heritage of both villages and architecture can be observed in the area. The wide variety of excellent local wineries can also be visited.

Western Australia

above The Pinnacles

Australia's biggest state, Western Australia covers a third of the island continent. It is larger than the whole of Western Europe, and four times the size of Texas, USA. The eastern border is a hot red desert, while the western border is hundreds of kilometres of beautiful coastline.

WESTERN AUSTRALIA
CITY

The capital of Western Australia is Perth, the city of the millionaires. The sunniest of all Australian cities, it has on average eight hours of sun each day. Perth nestles by a kilometre-wide expanse of the Swan River, and is edged by expensive suburbs and white sandy beaches.

Alf Curlewis Gardens
above
The Gardens overlook the modern skyscrapers of Perth whilst facing the river banks on the other side.

Swan Bells Tower
right
The Swan Bells include the twelve bells of St Martin-in-the-Fields, in existence since the late 13th century, and six new bells. The tower was built to house all 18 bells and to re-commemorate and re-celebrate many historic events. The bells are rung at regular intervals.

WESTERN AUSTRALIA
INLAND

Going inland into Western Australia offers the chance of exploring wilderness areas, mountain ranges, world renowned vineyards, forests, rivers, mining towns, caves, national parks, deserts and seemingly unending paddocks of wheat.

Ashburton River
The Ashburton flows 560 kilometres (348 miles) inland in the north-west region of Western Australia, and is the main river system in the Ashburton River Basin. It has a number of smaller rivers and creeks branching from the main channel. Its floodplains are mostly flat, wide and sediment filled, flowing only after seasonal rainfall or cyclone activity.

On the road to Moora
above
A dynamic wheat producing area north west of Perth

WESTERN AUSTRALIA | 41

WESTERN AUSTRALIA
COAST

The Western Australian coast stretches for miles on end, tracing the contours of half the country. It is recognized for its surfing beaches, islands, picturesque scenery and some rugged stretches.

Busselton Jetty, Busselton
above
The wooden jetty is over two kilometres in length and was restored after being damaged by Cyclone Alby in 1978.

Prevelly Beach
top
A popular spot for board riders near the Margaret River township

Pinnacles
left
Giant pinnacles rising from the sand, near Cervantes, north of Perth.

Margaret River
left
The Margaret River region is a rich dairy, cattle and timber region, but is better known Australia-wide for its production of excellent wines. It is also a popular holiday destination offering swimming, fishing and surfing. The Mammoth and Lake Caves are nearby.

Northern Territory

above The Devil's Marbles

The Territory covers one-sixth of Australia, and is divided into two regions, the Top End and the Red Centre. The Top End encapsulates the city of Darwin and its rugged coasts, whilst the Red Centre is home to the monolith Uluru (Ayres Rock), the 36 domes of Kata Tjuta (The Olgas) and the famous town of Alice Springs. This is true Outback country.

NORTHERN TERRITORY
INLAND

The inland is a blend of mining towns, furrowed land, square kilometres of bushland, national parks, unremitting desert, appeasing lagoons, and an abundance of Aboriginal culture.

Salt Water Crocodiles
Danger lurks around every corner in the Top End. Fifteen metre Saltwater Crocs are famous for their ferocious jaws.

Kangaroos
One of the highly recognized symbols of Australia is the native Kangaroo. The grey and red Kangaroos belong to the same family.

Katherine Gorge
left

Katherine Gorge is located in Nitmiluk National Park. The National Park is rich in Aboriginal art, with rock paintings representing the spiritual `dreaming' of the Jawoyn people, the traditional owners of the land.

Kakadu National Park

Comprising 8000 square miles of spectacular wildlife habitat, the Kakadu National Park has a range of high stone, plateau, forest woodland and monsoon rainforest. There are open savanna-like flood plains with billabongs, mangrove-fringed estuaries, plus the coastal beaches of the Arafura Sea.

Uluru (Ayers Rock)
top left

An amazing monolith in the middle of the Australian continent (465 kilometres - 290 miles - south-west of Alice Springs) on a flat plain of spinifex and other grasses. The traditional owners are the Anangu (Pitjantjatjara and Yantunytjatjara people) a number of whom live in the nearby Mutiljulu Community.

Kata Tjuta (The Olgas)
bottom left

Just 48 kilometres (30 miles) west of Uluru, and standing some 200 metres taller, are 36 individual domes known to the Anangu as Kata Tjuta — the place of many heads. This is a collection of giant weathered red domes with fissures, gorges and valleys carved between them, that are home to some captivating creatures of the region, such as the reptile the Thorny Devil.

Mount Connor
above

Mount Connor is a sprawling sandstone mesa about 90 kilometres (56 miles) east of Uluru. It is part of the Curtain Springs property. It can be climbed on the south side. The mount changes colours from soft pinks to dusky reds, depending on the time of day and year.

NORTHERN TERRITORY
CITY

Previously known as Stuart, the city of Alice Springs is the second largest town of the Northern Territory. It lies at the foot of the picturesque MacDonnell Ranges, in the geographic centre of the Australian Continent.

Alice Springs

With a population of 30,000, Alice Springs is Australia's premier Outback town. Some 1500 kilometres (932 miles) south of Darwin, and surrounded by ancient ranges and red desert, *The Alice* is now a modern city with a good shopping centre, very comfortable accommodation, and a good selection of entertainment venues. Everyone looks forward to the annual Henley on Todd, the only dry river regatta in the world.

NORTHERN TERRITORY
COAST

The northern coastline, mostly unspoiled, is sprawled with stretches of mangroves that cover one third of its coast, rocky headlands, pristine sandy beaches and remote reef systems.

Darwin

The relaxed capital of the Northern Territory is Darwin, a city of 109,419 people, located on Australia's far north-western coastline. It was a strategic outpost during World War II, and suffered tremendous damage during 64 air raids, with the loss of 243 lives. On Christmas Eve in 1974, Darwin was struck by one of the greatest natural disasters in Australian history, Cyclone Tracy, which left only approximately 500 of the city's then 8000 homes habitable.

Queensland

above Brisbane from the Brisbane River

Queensland, as the travel brochures say, is `beautiful one day, perfect the next'. A true tropical paradise, the state offers beautiful beaches, verdant rainforests, the stunning Outback, vibrant cities and a myriad of attractions. It is known as the Sunshine State.

QUEENSLAND
CITY

The capital of Queensland is Brisbane, which is situated on the banks of the Brisbane River. It boasts a sub-tropical climate and a very relaxed lifestyle.

Brisbane Parliament House
right
It was built in the settlement period and exhibits Renaissance style aesthetics. The building overlooks the Botanic Gardens.

Story Bridge
top right
The Story Bridge was Brisbane's answer to the Sydney Harbour Bridge. Built during the depression of the 1930s, it gave much needed work to many of the unemployed.

Captain Cook Bridge
bottom right
Flowing through the city, the Brisbane River is spanned by five bridges, all of which have their own unique style of architecture. The Captain Cook Bridge was built in 1972, and connects central Brisbane to Wooloongabba. It is majestic in size and looks its best at night.

QUEENSLAND INLAND

Inland Queensland is home to a fusion of true Outback country and dry bushlands on the one hand, and lush rainforests and mountain ranges on the other.

Windmill
right
Sunset in Outback Australia. The windmill driving the bore water to the surface is a symbol of the Outback and a water feature in an otherwise arid landscape.

Stockyard
below
Manning the gates of a stockyard in northern Queensland. The cattle industry is one of Australia's most important export earners.

QUEENSLAND COAST

The Queensland Coast consists of hundreds of pristine sandy white beaches, coral reefs and an abundance of sun.

Shute Harbour
below
Young explorers scavenge among rock pools in the sunny harbour. Mangrove trees are a familiar site in these parts of the coast.

Sunshine Coast

The Sunshine Coast stretches from Caloundra, north of Brisbane, to Double Island Point in the north. It boasts of 55 kilometres (34 miles) of white sandy beaches, such as Noosa (above).

Great Barrier Reef

The famous reef lies on the coastal edges of Northern Queensland. Beginning at Breaksea Spit, north of Bundaberg, it extends 2030 kilometres (1260 miles) north to the waters of New Guinea, making it the longest series of coral reefs and islands in the world. The reef is home to vast numbers of colourful species of fish and numerous varieties of corals.

Australian Capital Territory

Established in 1911, the independent capital territory was created out of political necessity free from domination by any one state. Gardens and parks surround the city.

left From Mount Ainslie looking down Anzac Parade to the Australian Parliament. This strip is regarded symbolically as the core of the nation.

above From the north side of Lake Burley Griffin looking to the Captain Cook Memorial Water Jet, with the National Library in the background.

AUSTRALIAN CAPITAL TERRITORY
CITY

Canberra is a garden city surrounded with a variation of shades and colours. It is the home of the Commonwealth Parliament.

Parliament House
above
Parliament House, in keeping with Walter Burley Griffin's original plan, is the central landmark of Canberra. While some might not be taken with the 81 metre (266 feet) stainless steel flagpole that dominates the city, all have to agree that the interior of the building is magnificent.

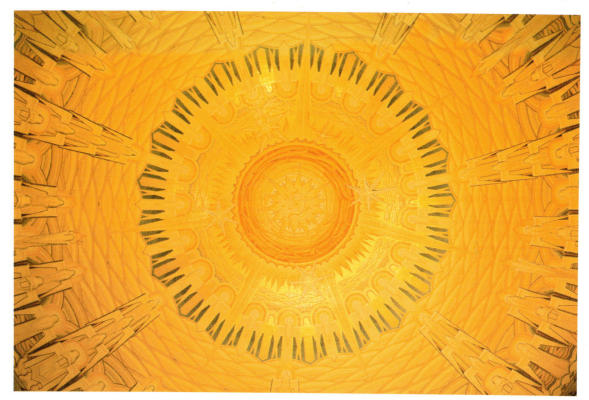

War Memorial, Canberra
above
The centre of the ceiling of the shrine in the Australian War Memorial, Canberra.

War Memorial, Canberra
right
An aspect of the surrounds of the Australian War Memorial, with relics from earlier conflicts.

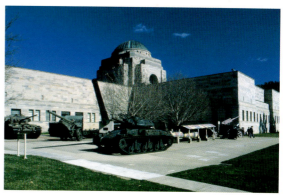

INDEX

A
Adelaide 34
Alice Springs 50
Ashburton River 41
Ayers Rock 48

B
Bogong High Plains 23
Brisbane
    Captain Cook Bridge 54
    Parliament House 54
    Story Bridge 54
Busselton Jetty 42
Byron Bay area 12

C
Canberra
    War Memorial 63
    Parliament Building 62
Clare Valley 37
Coles Bay 30
Crocodiles 46

D
Darling Harbour 9
Darwin 51
Devonport
    Mersey River 27

E
Echo Point 13

F
Freycinet National Park 29

G
Goulburn 5
Great Australian Bight 35
Great Barrier Reef 59

H
Hobart 26, 27

K
Kakadu National Park 46, 47
Kangaroo 46
Kata Tjuta 49
Katherine Gorge 47
Katoomba 13

M
Margaret River 43
McKenzie Falls 22
Melboure 17
    CBD 19
    Collins Street 19
    Kings Domain 20
    Princes Bridge 18
    Trams 18
Mount Arapiles 23
Mount Connor 49
Mount Field National Park 28
Mount Roland 28
Mount Wellington 26
Mt Olga 49

N
Nitmiluk National Park 47
Noosa 59

P
Paddington 9
Perth
    Alf Curlewis Gardens 40
    Swan Bells Tower 40
Pinnacles 38-39, 43
Port Phillips Bay 21
Prevelly Beach 42

S
Sandy Bay 30
Shute Harbour 58
South Australia Homestead 36
Stockyard 56
Sunshine Coast 59
Sydney
    City Centre 10
    Cockle Bay Wharf 9
    Department of lands building 10
    Harbour Bridge 7
    Hyde Park 10
    Opera House 8

T
Taronga Zoo 9
The Blue Mountains 13-14
The Devil's Marbles 44-45
Thredbo Creek 15
Twelve Apostles 21

U
Ulladulla Beach 12
Uluru 49

V
Victoria
    Countryside 23

W
Willunga township 36
Windmill 57

Acknowledgements

All images © Little Hills Press except

Colin Kerr
54

Northern Territory Tourist Commission
44-45, 50, 51

Tourism Victoria
17-18

Tourism Queensland
52-53